MW00652493

# Woman's Suffrage

## Researching American History

*edited by*

JoAnne Weisman Deitch

---

## Woman Suffrage
## is a
## Curse to Woman
## and a
## Danger to the State

---

*This sticker was issued by the National Association Opposed to Woman Suffrage, 1918.* (Courtesy of the National Archives)

Discovery Enterprises, Ltd.
Carlisle, Massachusetts

First Edition © Discovery Enterprises, Ltd., Carlisle, MA 2000

ISBN 1-57960-066-2

Library of Congress Catalog Card Number 00-191691

10  9  8  7  6  5  4  3  2  1

*Printed in the United States of America*

## Subject Reference Guide:

Title: *Woman's Suffrage*
Series: *Researching American History*
edited by JoAnne Weisman Deitch

Nonfiction
Analyzing documents re: Woman's Suffrage

## Credits:

*Cover illustration:* National Woman's Party suffragists demonstrating in front of the White House. (Courtesy of the National Woman's Party)

*Other illustrations:* Credited where they appear in the book.

## Special Thanks

Madeleine Meyers, for her research, editing, and introductory material which she prepared for *Forward into Light: The Struggle for Woman's Suffrage* (part of the *Perspectives on History Series* from Discovery Enterprises, Ltd.) much of which is included in this book.

# Contents

# About the Series

*Researching American History* is a series of books which introduces various topics and periods in our nation's history through the study of primary source documents.

## Reading the Historical Documents

On the following pages you'll find words written by people during or soon after the time of the events. This is firsthand information about what life was like back then. Illustrations are also created to record history. These historical documents are called **primary source materials**.

At first, some things written in earlier times may seem difficult to understand. Language changes over the years, and the objects and activities described might be unfamiliar. Also, spellings were sometimes different. Below is a model which describes how we help with these challenges.

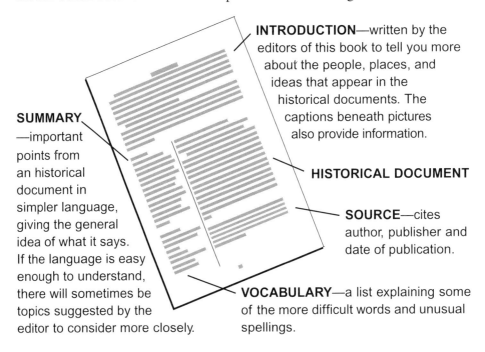

**INTRODUCTION**—written by the editors of this book to tell you more about the people, places, and ideas that appear in the historical documents. The captions beneath pictures also provide information.

**SUMMARY**—important points from an historical document in simpler language, giving the general idea of what it says. If the language is easy enough to understand, there will sometimes be topics suggested by the editor to consider more closely.

**HISTORICAL DOCUMENT**

**SOURCE**—cites author, publisher and date of publication.

**VOCABULARY**—a list explaining some of the more difficult words and unusual spellings.

In these historical documents, you may see three periods (…) called an ellipsis. It means that the editor has left out some words or sentences. You may see some words in brackets, such as [and]. These are words the editor has added to make the meaning clearer. When you use a document in a paper you're writing, you should include any ellipses and brackets it contains, just as you see them here. Be sure to give complete information about the author, title, and publisher of anything that was written by someone other than you.

# The Early Years

Early on in the American colonies, women had a subordinate status to the men in their lives, starting with their fathers, then their husbands, and sometimes, even their sons. They had almost total responsibility for domestic duties, such as maintaining the home, rearing the children, running the farm, and, of course, caring for their husbands—cooking, cleaning, laundering, and providing them with children. Women had no legal rights of their own, and everything that came with them to a marriage became the sole property of the husband. A colonial woman's own children legally belonged only to her husband.

During the early years in the colonies, women often felt frustrated by their lack of power, but were totally at their husbands' mercy as to whether they could even be heard on the subject.

## *Remember the Ladies*

In the colonies, women had been waiting a long time to have some attention paid to their concerns. As far back as March 31, 1776, Abigail Adams wrote to her husband, John, a prominent member of the Continental Congress, saying:

"…in the new Code of Laws which I suppose it will be necessary for you to make I desire you would Remember the Ladies, and be more generous and favourable to them than your ancestors. Do not put such unlimited power into the Hands of the Husbands. Remember all men would be tyrants if they could. If perticuliar care and attention is not paid to the Laidies we are determined to foment a Rebelion, and will not hold ourselves bound by any Laws in which we have no voice, or Representation."

Source: Abigail Adams, *Adams Family Correspondence,* Cambridge, MA: Belknap Press, 1963, p. 370.

**Summary:**
She asks her husband to keep women's rights in mind, otherwise women will rebel. They will not feel bound to honor a law for the creation of which they have had no input.

**Vocabulary:**
foment = stir up

*The image above, from a 19th century engraving, depicts a woman's life from cradle to grave. (Courtesy of* Constitution, *Vol. 7/No.1, NY, p. 48.)*

## *The Beginning of the "Rebelion"*

The official beginning of the "Rebelion" was at Seneca Falls, New York, on July 19 and 20, 1848. At that convention, women publicly expressed their dissatisfaction with their lack of legal rights. The demand for the right to vote was one of several resolutions approved by the women assembled at that convention, beginning a 72-year struggle for women's suffrage—one that would last until the passing of the 19th Amendment in August of 1920.

**Consider this:**

Why were the women the only ones allowed to speak on the first day of the convention?

**Vocabulary:**

deliberations = debates, discussions

### REPORT OF THE
### WOMAN'S RIGHTS CONVENTION,
*Held at SENECA FALLS, N. Y.,*
**July 19th and 20th, 1848.**

A CONVENTION to discuss the SOCIAL, CIVIL, AND RELIGIOUS CONDITION OF WOMAN, was called by the Women of Seneca County, N.Y., and held at the village of Seneca Falls, in the Wesleyan Chapel, on the 19th and 20th of July, 1848.

The question was discussed throughout two entire days: the first day by women exclusively, the second day men participated in the deliberations. LUCRETIA MOTT, of Philadelphia, was the moving spirit of the occasion.

. . . . . . . . . . . . . . . . . . . . . . . . . . . . . . . . . . . . . . .

## Declaration of Sentiments

When, in the course of human events, it becomes necessary for one portion of the family of man to assume among the people of the earth a position different from that which they have hitherto occupied, but one to which the laws of nature and of nature's God entitle them, a decent respect to the opinions of mankind requires that they should declare the causes that impel them to such a course.

We hold these truths to be self-evident; that all men and women are created equal; that they are endowed by their Creator with certain inalienable rights; that among these are life, liberty, and the pursuit of happiness; that to secure these rights governments are instituted, deriving their just powers from the consent of the governed. Whenever any form of Government becomes destructive of these ends, it is the right of those Who suffer from it to refuse allegiance to it, and to insist upon the institution of a new government, laying its foundation on such principles, and organizing its powers in such form as to them shall seem most likely to effect their safety and happiness.

. . . . . . . . . . . . . . . . . . . . . . . . . . . . . . . . . . . . . . .

The history of mankind is a history of repeated injuries and usurpations on the part of man toward woman, having in direct object the establishment of an absolute tyranny over her. To prove this, let facts be submitted to a candid world.

He has never permitted her to exercise her inalienable right to the elective franchise.

He has compelled her to submit to laws, in the formation of which she had no voice.

He has withheld from her rights which are given to the most ignorant and degraded men —both natives and foreigners.

**Summary:**

The speaker points out that when people have opposing opinions about the validity of an existing law or practice, it is their responsibility to express that opinion.

The speech continues with a variation of the Declaration of Independence, including the reference to "women." She goes on to describe the long history of man's authority over woman, and the lack of woman's rights.

**Vocabulary:**

allegiance = faithfulness
candid = frank, direct
degraded = dishonored
franchise = right or
   privilege
hitherto = until now,
   previously
impel = drive, push
inalienable = not to be
   transferred to another
Sentiments = opinions/
   beliefs
tyranny = power
usurpations = seizing of
   things

**Vocabulary:**

chastisement = punishment

civilly = as a citizen

covenant = contract, binding agreement

impunity = permission

mater = mother

monopolized = dominate by excluding others

remuneration = payment

scanty = meager

supposition = assumption

supremacy = power

Having deprived her of this first right of a citizen, the elective franchise, thereby leaving her without representation in the halls.

He has made her, if married, in the eye of the law, civilly dead.

He has taken from her all right in property, even to the wages she earns.

He has made her, morally, an irresponsible being, as she can commit many crimes with impunity, provided they be done in the presence of her husband. In the covenant of marriage, she is compelled to promise obedience to her husband, he becoming to all intents and purposes, her mater—the law giving him power to deprive her of her liberty, and to administer chastisement.

He has so framed the laws of divorce, as to what shall be the proper cause of divorce; in case of separation, to whom the guardianship of the children shall be given, as to be wholly regardless of the happiness of the woman —the law in all cases going upon the false supposition of the supremacy of the man, and giving all power into his hands.

After depriving her of all her rights as a married woman, if single and the owner of property, he has taxed her to support a government which recognizes her only when her property can be made profitable to it.

He has monopolized nearly all the profitable employments, and from those she is permitted to follow, she receives but a scanty remuneration.

He closes against her all the avenues to wealth and distinction, which he considers most honorable to himself. As a teacher of theology, medicine, or law, she is not known.

He has denied her the facilities for obtaining a thorough education—all colleges being closed against her.

He allows her in Church as well as State, but a subordinate Position, claiming Apostolic authority for her exclusion from the ministry, and, with some exceptions, from any public participation in the affairs of the Church.

He has created a false Public sentiment, by giving to the world a different code of morals for men and women, by which moral delinquencies which exclude women from society, are not only tolerated but deemed of little account in man.

. . . . . . . . . . . . . . . . . . . . . . . . . . . . . . . . . . .

He has endeavored, in every way that he could to destroy her confidence in her own Powers, to lessen her self-respect, and to make her willing to lead a dependant and abject life.

Now, in view of this entire disfranchisement of one-half the people of this country, their social and religious degradation,—in view of the unjust laws above mentioned, and because women do feel themselves aggrieved, oppressed, and fraudulently deprived of their most sacred rights, we insist that they have immediate admission to all the rights and privileges which belong to them as citizens of these United States.

In entering upon the great work before us, we anticipate no small amount of misconception, misrepresentation, and ridicule; but we shall use every instrumentality within our power to effect our object. We shall employ agents, circulate tracts, petition the State and national Legislatures, and endeavor to enlist the pulpit and the press in our behalf. We hope this Convention will be followed by a series of Conventions, embracing every part of the country.

Firmly relying upon the final triumph of the Right and the True, we do this day affix our signatures to this declaration.

**Summary:**
Women have been forced to depend upon men, who have done everything possible to undermine their self-confidence. As women gather to begin their fight for women's rights, even though they may be misrepresented and misunderstood by others, they will do everything in their power to obtain equality.

The *Declaration of Sentiments* is signed by those present.

**Vocabulary:**
abject = wretched, miserable
aggrieved = offended
degradation = disgrace
deprived of = denied
disfranchisement = depriving people of the right to vote
endeavored = tried
fraudulently = unlawfully, or based on fraud
misconception = a wrong interpretation
of little account = not important
oppressed = overwhelmed, persecuted
subordinate = lower level

# Women Speak out around the Country

After the word spread about the Seneca Falls Convention (which had primarily drawn women from upper state New York), women from around the country gathered to reinforce the work of their peers, and gain courage from each other. Many of these same women had been involved in the abolitionist movement, and had already made their anti-slavery opinions known. In October 1850, a national women's conference was held in Worcester, Massachusetts. It was to be the first of the annual national conventions for years to come. This convention, unlike that in Seneca Falls, resulted in the first standing committees organized to work for women's rights.

The suffragists' activities slowed during the years of the Civil War, but many of the same women worked actively for abolition. Wendall Phillips, a prominent abolitionist of the time, warned women: "One question at a time. This hour belongs to the Negro."

## *Worcester, Massachusetts Holds Women's Convention*

Along with speaking out on woman's suffrage and equal education at the Worcester Conference, October 1850, a tribute to women slaves was voiced, and their inclusion in the women's efforts for equal rights was promised:

**Summary:**
As we gather to work towards women's rights, we remember the women who are slaves. The women here will work for the rights of those slaves, as well as for their own rights.

**Vocabulary:**
advocate = recommend
grossly = glaringly

Resolved, That the cause we are met to advocate, —the claim for woman of all her natural and civil rights,—bids us remember the million and a half of slave women at the South, the most grossly wronged and foully outraged of all women; and in every effort for an improvement in our civilization, we will bear in our heart of hearts the memory of the trampled womanhood of the plantation, and omit no effort to raise it to a share in the rights we claim for ourselves.

Source: Worcester Women's Convention, October 1850. Found on website WWWomen.com.

### Sojourner Truth

Sojourner Truth was born into slavery in New York in 1795, and gained her freedom in 1827, when the state emancipated its slaves. After working as a domestic for several years, she began to speak publicly on behalf of abolition and the rights of women. In 1851, she attended a women's convention in Akron, Ohio. The convention participants did not support her attendance; they were afraid that their cause, the rights of women, would be [compromised] if it were associated with the rights of blacks. Sojourner Truth rose from her seat and approached the platform.

— Professor E.D. Hirsch Jr.
*The Lowell Sun*

### Ain't I A Woman?
### Sojourner Truth Speaks Out
**spoken by Sojourner Truth at the**
**Women's Convention in Akron, Ohio, 1851**

Well, children, there is so much racket there must be something out of kilter. I think that 'twixt the Negroes of the South and the women of the North, all talking about rights, the white men will be in a fix pretty soon. But what's all this talking about? That man over there says that women need to be helped into carriages, and lifted over ditches, and to have the best place

**Summary:**

From the Negroes in the South to the women in the North, everyone is talking about rights.

**Vocabulary:**

out of kilter = not in good condition

'twixt = shortened form of betwixt, between

**Summary:**

White women are treated politely and are helped by men, but the Negro women are not. Aren't I a woman too?

Some may think that I may not be as smart as a white woman, but I'm still entitled to have rights.

Men shouldn't act so superior; afterall, Jesus Christ was created by God and a woman—man had nothing to do with it.

everywhere. Nobody helps me into carriages, or over mud puddles, or gives me any best place! Ain't I a woman? Look at me! Look at my arm! I have ploughed and planted, and gathered into barns, and no man could head me! And ain't I a woman? I could work as much and eat as much as man—when I could get it—and bear the lash as well!

And ain't I a woman? I have borne 13 children, and seen them most all sold off to slavery, and when I cried out with my mother's grief, none but Jesus heard me! And ain't I a woman?

Then they talk about this thing in my head; what's this they call it? (Intellect, someone whispers.) That's it, honey. What's that got to do with women's rights or Negroes' rights?

If my cup won't hold but a pint, and yours holds a quart, wouldn't you be mean not to let me have my half-measure full? Then that little man in black there, he says women can't have as much rights as men, 'cause Christ wasn't a woman!

From God and woman! Man had nothing to do with Him! If the first woman God ever made was strong enough to turn the world upside down all alone, these women together ought to be able to turn it back, and get it right side up again! And now they is asking to do it, the men better let them. Obliged to you for hearing me, and now old Sojourner Truth ain't got nothing more to say.

Source: Sojourner Truth, Women's Convention in Akron, Ohio, 1851. Found in: *Sojourner Truth fights back at convention*, edited and introduced by Professor E.D. Hirsch Jr., Lowell, MA: *The Sun*, February 28, 1993.

# A Mormon Woman Reveals Voting Practices

Women all over the country were becoming increasingly dissatisfied with the voting situation. Even though Utah was not yet admitted to the Union at the time, outspoken Mormon Fannie Stenhouse registered her complaints and exposed the Mormons' peculiar voting practices in her controversial autobiography, excerpted below.

## A Wagon-Load of Lady Voters!

…It will be a matter of interest to the advocates of women's suffrage to learn that Brigham Young conferred the franchise upon the Mormon ladies. This, at first, appears to be a very liberal measure; but let not the innocent reader be deceived thereby. The opening of the mines and the great influx of Gentiles, consequent upon the completion of the Union Pacific Railroad, proved very clearly to Brigham that the day might come when the Gentiles would have an equality, if not a majority, of votes, and in that day the slavish despotism of the Mormon Priesthood would be overthrown. The time, certainly, was very far off, but it was wise to provide for contingencies. So a bill was brought in conferring upon women the privilege of voting. No Mormon woman would for a moment ever dream of voting otherwise than she was directed by her husband, and no man would think of voting except as he was "counselled" by the Priesthood. Thus, a man with half a dozen wives would now have half a dozen votes, and Brother Brigham, instead of having only his own single vote, would have nineteen for his nineteen wives, to say nothing of his daughters and the whole array of spiritual wives which he might produce. I have often seen one solitary man driving into the City a whole wagon-load of women of all ages and sizes— they were going to the poll, and their votes

**Summary:**

Brigham Young, the leader of the Mormons, allowed women to vote so that as more non-Mormons moved to Utah, the Church would not lose its majority power. But no Mormon woman would dare to vote her own conscience. Rather, she would vote as her husband directed her. He, of course, would be directed by Church leaders on how to vote. Therefore, a man with many wives [polygamy was a common pactice by Mormons of the time] would get many votes.

**Vocabulary:**

advocates = people who speak in favor of something

conferring = bestowing an honor

contingencies = possibilities

despotism = rule by an absolute power

franchise = right to vote

Gentiles = to Mormons, anyone who is not a Mormon

**Summary:**

With this practice in place, women actually had no benefit from their votes.

**Vocabulary:**

fetters = restraints

would be one! It is very easy to see how in this way the influence of the Priesthood has been extended, and women themselves have been made the instruments for rivetting still more firmly their own fetters. But it is by no means easy to see that women in Utah have derived any benefit from being permitted to vote.

Source: Fannie Stenhouse, *Tell It All: The Story of a Life's Experience in Mormonism. An Autobiography by Mrs. T. B. H. Stenhouse, of Salt Lake City, For More Than Twenty Years The Wife of a Mormon Missionary and Elder,* Hartford, Conn.: A. D. Worthington & Co., Publishers. Queen City Publishing Co., Cincinnati. Excelsior Publishing Co., St. Louis, 1875, pp 606-7. Found on Making of America website: http://moa.umd/.umich.edu/ index.html.

# Susan B. Anthony Joins the Cause

Susan B. Anthony, a Quaker teacher who had resigned her position in protest against discrimination toward women, was ready and eager to fight for reform. She and Elizabeth Cady Stanton took up the suffrage cause, often working together, with great vigor. They soon became the most recognized and inspiring leaders of the cause, along with Lucretia Mott and Lucy Stone.

## Susan B. Anthony Springs into Action

The passing of the 14th Amendment in 1868 included the word "male" for the first time in the U. S. Constitution. This was a major setback for the suffragists, and they didn't take it lightly. When Anthony read an editorial in a Rochester, New York paper, she sprang into action. Following the editorial below are Anthony's letter to Elizabeth Cady Stanton, a letter to the *New York Times* in response, several short excerpts from Anthony's diary, and a *New York Times* account of Anthony's trial.

Now Register? To-day and to-morrow are the only remaining opportunities. If you were not permitted to vote, you would fight for the right, undergo all privations for it, face death for it. You have it now at the cost of five minutes' time to be spent in seeking your place of registration, and having your name entered. And yet, on election day, less than a week hence, hundreds of you are likely to lose your votes because you have not thought it worth while to give the five minutes. To-day and to-morrow are your only opportunities. Register now!

Source: *The Democrat and Chronicle*, Rochester, New York, Nov. 1, 1872. Found in *Forward into Light: The Struggle for Woman's Suffrage*, Madeleine Meyers, editor, Carlisle, MA: Discovery Enterprises, Ltd., 1994, p. 31.

**Summary:**
She urges women to register to vote in the next two days, so they won't waste their right to vote on election day.

**Vocabulary:**
hence = from now
privations = lack of the basic necessities of life

She immediately wrote to Elizabeth Cady Stanton to tell her what she had done.

**Summary:**

Susan B. Anthony voted the Republican ticket. She reports on others who registered and those who weren't permitted to register.

She was happy to read of other suffrage news in the Hartford newspapers that Elizabeth Cady Stanton had sent.

**Vocabulary:**

ditto = the same as before

eloquent = well spoken, persuasive

Rochester Nov. 5th 1872

Dear Mrs Stanton

Well I have been & gone & done it!!—positively voted the Republican ticket—strait—this A.M. at 7 o' clock & swore my vote in at that—was registered on Friday & 15 other women followed suit in this ward—then in sundry others some 20 or thirty other women tried to register, but all save two were refused—all my three sisters voted—Rhoda De Garmo—too—Amy Post was rejected—she will immediately bring action against the registrars—then another woman who was registered but vote refused will bring action for that—similar to the Washington action. Hon Henry R. Selden will be our counsel—he has read up the law & all of our arguments & is satisfied that we are right & ditto the judge Samuel Selden—his elder brother—so we are in for a fine agitation in Rochester on the question.

I hope the morning's telegrams will tell of many women all over the county trying to vote—It is splendid that without any concert of action so many should have moved here.

Thanks for the Hartford Papers.—What a magnificient meeting you had—splendid climax of the campaign—the two ablest & most eloquent women on one platform—& the Gov. of the state by your side—I was with you in spirit that evening, the Chairman of the Committee had both telegraphed & written me all about the arrangements—

Haven't we wedged ourselves into the work pretty fairly & fully—& now that the Republicans have taken our votes—for it is the Republican members of the Board—the Democratic paper is out against us strong—& that scared the Democrats on the registry board—

How I wish you were here to write of the funny things said & done—Rhoda De Garmo told them she wouldn't swear nor affirm—but would tell them the truth—& they accepted that. When the Democrats said my vote should not go in the box—one Republican said to the other—What do you say Marsh?—I say put it in!—So do I said Jones—and— "We'll fight it out on this live if it takes all winter." —Mary Hollowell was just here—she & Mrs Millis tried to register but were refused.—also Mrs Mann the Unitarian Minister's wife—& Mary Curtiss, —sister of Catharine Stebbins—not a jeer not a word—not a look disrespectful has met a single woman—

If only now—all the Woman Suffrage women would work to this end of enforcing the existing constitution supremacy of national law over state law—what strides we might make this very winter—But—I'm awful tired—for five days I have been on the constant run —but to splendid purpose—so all right—I hope you voted too—

affectionately Susan B. Anthony

Source: Madeleine Meyers, editor, *Forward into Light: The Struggle for Woman's Suffrage*, Carlisle, MA: Discovery Enterprises, Ltd., 1994, pp. 31-3.

**Summary:**

She goes on the explain that the Republicans allowed women to register, but the Democrats were opposed to it. Those who were denied the right to register have obtained a lawyer to help them.

**Vocabulary:**

affirm = to declare formally

supremacy = authority

In response to Stanton's views on suffrage and Anthony's registration, "a woman" states her views on suffrage in a letter to the editor of the *New York Times*.

**Summary:**

She believes that most women would rather not have the right to vote.

**Vocabulary:**

abhor = hate
aloof = apart
ascertain = determine
computation = figuring
incumbent upon = resting
    upon, relying on

To the Editor of the *New York Times*:

May I ask you to give me space for a few words? I have this morning read Mrs. E. C. Stanton's communication on the subject of Miss Anthony's case, now before the courts, and I cannot refrain from saying a word to these ladies. Have they, while working so earnestly for the enfranchisement of women, an idea of how the majority of their countrywomen feel on the subject? I believe, from all that I have ever been able to ascertain, that for every one woman who desires to vote, there are ten at the least computation who do not wish to do so. And are we, the majority of educated women in this country, to have political duties thrust upon us, which we not only do not desire, but utterly abhor! In our hatred of publicity, in our desire to keep utterly aloof from a matter which is so distasteful to us, we have said too little, have kept silence too long, until the strong-minded party think we care nothing about it. Could I speak with a thousand tongues, it would be to give a hundred thousand reasons why we should not vote. We can use our influence in our homes, a woman's proper sphere, and who can tell how much we do use it now! It is all we want. Let almost any woman who has a family to care for speak, and say how much time she has to devote to the study of political questions, and to the duties which are incumbent upon voters; for if we are made voters, we are in honor bound to fulfill to the utmost all the duties attached to the so-called "privilege." ...To the women of our land who yet love their own womanly sphere, I say, Keep silence in public when you can; but work, work at home in your own dominion, that we may be saved from this fate. I hope, and I know that I speak for many besides myself in saying this, that for many years to come there may be found men enough who care for the peace, dignity, modesty, and womanly reserve of their mothers, wives, daughters, and sisters to protect us from having thrust upon us that dreaded "right" of voting.

A Woman.<br>
No. 461 West Twenty-third Street,<br>
New York, Thursday, Jan. 30, 1873.

Source: *New York Times*, February 3, 1873. Found in *Forward into Light: The Struggle for Woman's Suffrage*, Madeleine Meyers, editor, Carlisle, MA: Discovery Enterprises, Ltd., 1994, pp. 34-5.

**Summary:**
She urges women to be quiet in public life and influence the vote at home.

Excerpts from the diary of Susan B. Anthony.

**Consider this:**

Anthony's diary consists of short phrases with many abbreviations and little punctuation. Choose a day and rewrite the diary in full sentences.

Vocabulary:
deferred = postponed, delayed
sublime = awe-inspiring

*June Wednesday, 18 1873*

Circuit Court—judge Hunt refused judge S. to address jury—& instructed jury to bring in verdict of guilty—& refused to poll jury—Inspector's convicted & Van Voorhis denied address to jury—The greatest outrage history ever witnessed—

*June Thursday, 19*

Mrs Hebbard, Mosher, Leyden, Anthony, Pulver came down to Cand.—New trial moved by both Selden & Van V.—hearing at 2. P.M.—masterly statements of cause by both S. & V.—judge H. denied my case at once—deferred Inspectors till morning—Att. moved my sentence—judge asked reason why sentence should not be. I answered—

I have much to say—A sublime silence reigned in court while I declared every right stricken down—

*June Friday, 20*

Mrs Gage went home—& so did I—but Friday A.M. found me in court again, bound to stand by & see the Inspectors through. V's pleas were clear & unanswerable but no law, logic or justice could change his will. We were convicted before hearing & all trial a mere farce—

Source: The Diary of Susan B. Anthony. Found in *Forward into Light: The Struggle for Woman's Suffrage*, Madeleine Meyers, editor, Carlisle, MA: Discovery Enterprises, Ltd., 1994, pp. 35-6.

The following article appeared in the *New York Times*, June 20, 1873.

### Miss Susan B. Anthony Fined $100 and Costs for Illegal Voting

CANANDAIGUA, N.Y., June 19.-At 2 o'clock this afternoon Judge Selden made a motion in the case of Miss Anthony for a new trial, upon the ground of a misdirection of the judge in ordering a verdict of guilty without submitting the case to the jury. He maintained, in an elaborate argument, the right of every person charged with crime to have the question of guilt or innocence passed upon by a constitutional jury, and that there was no power in this court to deprive her of it.

The District Attorney replied, when the Court, in a brief review of the argument of the counsel, denied the motion.

The District Attorney immediately moved that the judgment of the Court be pronounced upon the defendant.

The Court made the usual inquiry of Miss Anthony if she had anything to say why sentence should not be pronounced.

Miss Anthony answered and said she had a great many things to say, and declared that in her trial every principle of justice had been violated; that every right had been denied; that she had had no trial by her peers; that the Court and the jurors were her political superiors and not her peers, and announced her determination to continue her labors until equality was obtained, and was proceeding to discuss the question involved in the case, when she was interrupted by the Court with the remark that these questions could not be reviewed.

Miss Anthony replied she wished it fully understood that she asked no clemency from

**Summary:**

The Judge made a motion for a new trial, because Anthony's case had not been submitted to a jury.

When the Court denied the motion, Anthony stated that every principle of justice had been violated in this case.

21

**Summary:**

The judge then fined her $100, and the trial ended.

**Vocabulary:**
clemency = forgiveness
prosecution = legal
  proceeding
rigor = sterness

the Court; that she desired and demanded the full rigor of the law.

Judge Hunt then said the judgment of the Court is that you pay a fine of $100 and the costs of the prosecution, and immediately added, there is no order that you stand committed until the fine is paid; and so the trial ended.

A motion for a new trial is to be made in the case of the inspectors to-morrow morning on the ground that Hall, one of the defendants, was absent during the trial.

Source: The *New York Times*, June 20, 1873. Found in *Forward into Light: The Struggle for Woman's Suffrage*, Madeleine Meyers, editor, Carlisle, MA: Discovery Enterprises, Ltd., 1994, pp. 36-7.

Susan B. Anthony was fined $100, which she refused to pay. She was never penalized for this, nor were the other women brought to trial.

# Song of Anti-Suffrage

Expressions of opinions about suffrage varied as much in style as they did in stance. Many songs were written for and against the women's desire to gain the vote. One song popular with anti-suffragists follows.

### Female Suffrage
#### by R.A. Cohen

You may wear your silks and satin,
    Go when and where you please,
Make embroidery and tattin',
    And live quite at your ease.
You may go to ball and concert,
    In gaudy hat and coat—
In fact, my charming creatures,
    Do everything but vote.

    [Repeat *Chorus* after every verse:]
You may visit ball and concert,
    In gaudy hat and coat,
    In fact, my charming creatures,
    Do everything but vote.

You may seek for health and riches,
    And marry at your will,
But man must wear the breeches,
    And rule the household still;
For nature so designed it,
    And so our fathers wrote,
    And clearly they defined it,
That man, alone, should vote. *Chorus*

Then mothers, wives and sisters,
    I beg you keep your place;
And remain what nature made you—The
    help-meets of our race.
Let no temptation lead you,
    Nor any wily fox,
To descend unto the level Of the nation's
    ballot-box. *Chorus*

Source: Original sheet music, St. Joseph, Missouri: P.L. Huyett & Son, 1867. Found in *Songs America Voted By*, by Irwin Silber, Stackpole Books, 1977, p. 229, verses 1, 2, and 6.

**Activity:**
Analyze this song using the worksheet on page 55.

# Suffrage Groups Formed

(Courtesy of the National Archives)

In the years that followed, two suffragist groups approached social reform with different platforms. Lucy Stone, Julia Ward Howe, and Henry Blackwell took the reigns of the American Woman Suffrage Association (AWSA), to work for the passing of the 15th Amendment, prohibiting state and federal government from denying anyone the vote based on "race, color, or previous condition of servitude." A group which was headed by Susan Anthony and Elizabeth Cady Stanton, the National Woman Suffrage Association (NWSA) was totally committed to women's rights. The two worked on and on for years. Finally, in 1890, when Wyoming applied for statehood, it became the first state with woman's suffrage. Colorado (1893), Utah, and Idaho (1896) followed. After years of competition, the two major suffragist groups joined together, forming the National American Woman Suffrage Association (NAWSA).

## *New Century, New Leaders*
by Madeleine Meyers

By the beginning of the 20th century Susan B. Anthony and Elizabeth Cady Stanton were both in their eighties, and Lucretia Mott was dead. Anthony recognized the need for younger women to take the lead in the move-ment. At the convention of the National American Woman Suffrage Associa-tion held in Washington, D. C. in 1900, she brought forward Carrie Chapman Catt to be the new president. Catt had spent many years working in the field, and for the past five years had been the head of the Organization Committee. Her ability to organize and talent at public speaking made her a natural leader.

# Parading for Votes

Between 1910 and 1920 women captured the attention of the nation by parading for votes. Although most of the parades were peaceful, a few were not. The accounts which follow give the flavor of the marches.

## *Suffrage Army Out On Parade*

Ten thousand strong, the army of those who believe in the cause of woman's suffrage marched up Fifth Avenue at sundown yesterday in a parade the like of which New York never knew before. Dusty and weary, the marchers went to their homes last night satisfied that their year of hard work in preparing for the demonstration had borne good fruit.

It was an immense crowd that came out to stand upon the sidewalks to cheer or jeer.... It was a crowd that took every inch of the sidewalk from Washington Square to Carnegie Hall, that filled all the steps and crowded all the windows along the line of march....

### The Start of the Parade

Promptly at 5 o'clock...the order to start the parade came.... Then a company of women on horseback trotted smartly around the east side of Washington Arch, and the great suffrage parade had begun.... It took the entire line one hour and fifty-five minutes to pass....

### Sharp Contrasts Among the Marchers

It was a parade of contrasts—contrasts among women. There were women of every occupation and profession, and women of all ages, from those so advanced in years that they had to ride in carriages down to suffragettes so small that they were pushed along in perambulators. There were women whose faces bore traces of a life of hard work and many

**Consider this:**
Describe some of the contrasts mentioned, in your own words.

**Vocabulary:**
perambulators = baby carriages

25

**Consider this:**

Why would the reporter have condidered the men's division the most exciting or impressive?

worries. There were young girls, lovely of face and fashionably gowned. There were motherly looking women, and others with the confident bearing obtained from contact with the business world.

There were women who smiled in a preoccupied way as though they had just put the roast into the oven, whipped off their aprons and hurried out to be in the parade. They were plainly worried at leaving their household cares for so long, yet they were determined to show their loyalty to the cause. There were women who marched those weary miles who had large bank accounts. There were slender girls, tired after long hours of factory work. There were nurses, teachers, cooks, writers, social workers, librarians, school girls, laundry workers. There were women who work with their heads, and women who work with their hands, and women who never work at all. And they all marched for suffrage.

### The Men's Division

But the real excitement, the real moment in the parade, for which many of the spectators had waited since noon, was the delegation of men. If there were women of every sort, there were men of every sort, and their number, grown tremendously from the scanty and much-derided eighty of last year, was close to a thousand. Some said that there were more than two thousand, but these estimates were much too large. There were men with gray hair, who lifted their silk hats with an old-school courtliness in response to the chorus from the sidewalk which bewildered them, and which they did not exactly understand. There were young men fashionably dressed, and some men of prominence in the city who swung into the parade yesterday....

26

## Women Mostly Dressed in White

Most of the women, particularly the younger women, were dressed all in white, except for the outflashing of yellow and purple and green and red that was in the ribbons they wore, the banners they carried, and the flags they waved. And many of the women wore the suffrage hat, trimmed to suit their own taste.… There were women, too, in great numbers who came in their regular street dress or gowned as they were when they quit work, to march for the cause.

## Children Cheer Their Teachers

The teachers, followed by pretty school girls innumerable, joined the parade from Washington Square.… Their banners commented caustically on the illiteracy of children under the rule of man. … And from the sidewalks there was a running chorus of amusement and delight as the school children caught sight of their teachers in the line of march.

Source: *New York Times*, May 5, 1912, p. 1. Found in *Forward into Light: The Struggle for Woman's Suffrage*, Madeleine Meyers, editor, Carlisle, MA: Discovery Enterprises, Ltd., 1994, pp. 38-43.

**Consider this:**
This is a very vivid description of the participants. Have you ever been to a political parade or rally? Describe what you saw, in person, or choose a similar event that you saw on the TV news to describe.

**Vocabulary**:
caustically = with a biting wit

Parades were held in cities and towns all over the country. When things got tough for the marchers in the nation's capital in March of 1913, the following report in the *New York Times* was published.

## *Parade Protest Arouses Senate*

WASHINGTON. March 4.—Bitter complaint was heard on every hand today because of the lack of protection given to the women marchers by the Metropolitan Police during the suffrage pageant and procession yesterday. Congress had passed a special resolution directing that Pennsylvania Avenue be kept clear for the demonstration. Many persons were injured.

**Consider this:**
During the Washington march the police were criticized for not protecting the marchers. Can you think of a recent case where the same kind of complaint was voiced? Describe it.

**Consider this:**

The police often have a difficult time with crowd control at political events and social reform rallies.

The public relies on police supervision, but often criticizes the police for being too lenient or too tough.

In your own research find examples where this has been a problem. Were the police too lenient or too harsh? Explain.

The stories of the police do not agree. One policeman said yesterday that the police authorities had no idea that they would have to handle the tremendous crowd, equal to any inauguration gathering that flocked into Pennsylvania Avenue yesterday and had not detailed enough men for that reason. Leaders in the suffrage cause say that those policemen who were detailed did not perform their duty....

"I do not want to be unfair," said Mrs. Glenna S. Tinnan of Washington, the director of the pageant, "but the treatment accorded us was simply unspeakable. It was more than a question of an undermanned police line. Those who were assigned to the task not only did little or nothing, but even seemed to encourage the hoodlums in the work of breaking up the parade."...

"Only one policeman that I saw did his full duty. Some stood in groups and twiddled their fingers and repeated again and again, 'We can do nothing with this crowd.' I heard another policeman say, 'If my wife were in that line of march I'd knock her down.'...

"The Boy Scouts," said Miss Alice Paul of Philadelphia. "were the only ones who did any effective police work."

Source: *New York Times*, March 5, 1913, p. 8. Found in *Forward into Light: The Struggle for Woman's Suffrage*, Madeleine Meyers, editor, Carlisle, MA: Discovery Enterprises, Ltd., 1994, pp. 46-7.

# Silent Sentinels

by Madeleine Meyers

*Miss Alice Paul, chair of the National Woman's Party.*

By 1914 the more traditional National American Woman Suffrage Association had split with a group of women, led by Alice Paul, who believed that they should hold whichever party was in power responsible for passing the woman's suffrage amendment. This group became the National Woman's Party, and in 1917 began a campaign of peacefully picketing outside the White House, a right they were assured was legal. Many of the signs they carried displayed President Wilson's own words about democracy. *(See cover photo.)*

President Wilson and Envoy Root are deceiving Russia. They say "We are a democracy. Help us to win the war so that democracies may survive." We women of America tell you that America is not a democracy. Twenty million women are denied the right to vote. President Wilson is the chief opponent of their national enfranchisement. Help us make this nation really free. Tell our government that it must liberate its people before it can claim free Russia as an ally.

Source: Leaflet written and distributed by Alice Paul outside of the White House in 1917.

**Consider this:**

Can a country consider itself a democracy if one half of its citizens are denied the right to vote?

For the first few months the women were allowed to picket peacefully; however, attitudes changed after the U.S. entered World War I in April. In June, after a banner addressed to a visiting official from Russia was deemed an embarrassment, the women began to be arrested for obstructing traffic. Before this sad chapter was over, women had been sent to the Occoquan Workhouse, forcibly fed, and, in Alice Paul's case, even put in a ward for the insane.

On November 27 and 28, 1917, all of the women were suddenly released. Some of the women appealed their original sentences, and in March, 1918, it was decided that there had been no just cause to arrest the women. Since all of the pickets had been arrested on the same charge, all of the arrests were therefore invalid. For that reason, the District of Columbia was ordered to bear all of the costs of the trials.

The following section includes descriptions of the picketing, imprisonments, a poem that grew out of the movement, and some opinions generated by the picketing.

*Men gathered outside the Anti-Suffrage Headquarters.* (Courtesy of the National Archives)

*The Cut Direct*

### Suffragists Wait at the
### White House for Action

There is a royal blaze of color at the White House gates these nipping winter days. Across Lafayette Square, through the lovely tracery of bare trees, the cold classic lines of the White House have receded into their winter background. Instead a gallant display of purple, white and gold banners through the trees holds the eye. They are like trumpet calls. Many were caught by the lovely sight last week when the suffrage pickets of the Congressional Union first went on guard at the White House. For the first time in history the President of these United States is being picketed, is being waited upon day after day by representatives of the women of the nation, is being asked a question that must finally be answered to the nation.

**Summary:**

There is a blaze of color at the White House, despite the winter scene. Gold and purple banners are being displayed by the suffragette pickets.

**Vocabulary:**

pickets = demonstrators, usually holding a sign or banner with a political message

**Summary:**

The banners address President Wilson on woman's suffrage issues, which are being expressed all over the country.

**Vocabulary:**

demure = prim, modest
flanking = along-side
rank and file = crowds, the masses
sentinels = guards

Many walked across Lafayette Square the day the banners first called, to look at the unusual sight in front of that dignified place that is each day visited by people from every part of the country. Flanking the impressive east and west gates of the White House were merely twelve young women, holding high floating purple, white and gold banners. The young women were demure and unsmiling and silent.

…the questions that those lettered banners are day after day asking, men and women are echoing and re-echoing across the nation. "Mr. President, what are you going to do about woman's suffrage?" "Mr. President, how long must women wait for liberty?" The fact is that thousands of men and women of this nation because of those silent sentinels with their purple, white and gold standards, have asked themselves for the first time, "What is the President doing about federal suffrage? What could he do? Why is he not doing it?" From every section of the country these voices of the great rank and file that make public opinion are being expressed in the press of the country. Never before has a picket organized to call attention to a wrong excited more comment, resounded over farther territory.

Source: *The Suffragist*, January 17, 1917.

*Women picketing outside the White House.* (Smithsonian)

### *On the Picket Line*
by Beulah Amidon

The avenue is misty gray,
And here beside the guarded gate
We hold our golden blowing flags
And wait.

The people pass in friendly wise;
They smile their greeting where we stand
And turn aside to recognize
The just demand.

Often the gates are swung aside:
The man whose power could free us now
Looks from his car to read our plea—
And bow.

Sometimes the little children laugh;
The careless folk toss careless words,
And scoff and turn away, and yet
The people pass the whole long day
Those golden flags against the gray
And can't forget.

Source: *The Suffragist*, March 3, 1917.

**Activity:**

Rewrite this poem as prose.

Evalute this poem using the worksheet on page 55.

**Consider this:**

The author of this article suggests that the women were arrested on false charges. Do you agree?

Where does the Constitution protect our right to free speech and the right to demonstrate peacefully?

**Vocabulary:**

baffle = puzzle

grotesque = bizarre, outlandish

precipitated = unexpectedly occuring

# Women Arrested

Sixteen women, representing the states of the West, the East and the South, during the past week have been arrested for the peace-picketing of the White House. Beginning with a riot which was precipitated by the action of the police, the grotesque chapter which this week adds to the fifty-years' battle for suffrage will baffle future students of the movement in this country....

...The picket went out as usual Friday, June 22, when Miss Lucy Burns and Miss Katherine Morey stood at the lower gates of the White House with the familiar banner carrying the President's own words:

"We will fight for the things we have always held nearest our hearts, for democracy, for the right of those who submit to authority to have a voice in their own governments."

For seven minutes the police pondered. "We can't arrest the President's message," they said, "they've had it out before." Then they took a chance and obeyed orders. Technically Miss Burns and Miss Morey found they were arrested for "obstructing traffic," though there had been no traffic at the time of their arrest, and Inspector Grant and Major Pullman seemed embarrassed and unable to explain the new ruling.

Source: *The Suffragist*, June, 1917.

### "That Night of Terror"
November 14, 1917
As Described by Mrs. Mary A. Nolan

I was giving all my time to Red Cross work in the surgical department of the Jacksonville (Florida) Branch when I first heard of Alice Paul—that they had put her in prison with those others. They were suffering and fighting for all of us. When Mrs. Gould and Miss Younger asked Florida women to go to Washington to help, I volunteered. I am seventy-three, but except for my lame foot I was well. . . .

I picketed three times with these splendid women, carrying a purple, white and gold suffrage flag. The third time we spent the night in the House of Detention because we refused to give bail. . . .

They ran through that "trial" rapidly the next day. We did not answer them or pay any attention. We knew, of course, that we would all be convicted and sentenced for months, just as the hundred and more other women who had done this thing for suffrage.

It was about half past seven at night when we got to Occoquan workhouse. A woman was standing behind a desk when we were brought into this office, and there were six men also in the room. Mrs. Lewis, who spoke for all of us, refused to talk to the woman—who, I learned, was Mrs. Herndon—and said she must speak to Mr. Whittaker, the superintendent of the place. . . .

Suddenly the door literally burst open and Whittaker rushed in like a tornado; some men followed him. We could see the crowds of them on the porch. They were not in uniform. They looked as much like tramps as anything. They seemed to come in-and in-and in. One had a

**Consider this:**

Show examples of Mrs. Nolan's description of the events which would enrage a reader sympathetic to her cause.

face that made me think of an orang-outang. Mrs. Lewis stood up—we had been sitting and lying on the floor; we were so tired but she had hardly begun to speak, saying we demanded to be treated as political prisoners when Whittaker said:

"You shut up! I have men here glad to handle you. Seize her!" I just saw men spring toward her and someone screamed, "They have taken Mrs. Lewis," when a man sprang at me, and caught me by the shoulder. I am used to being careful of my bad foot and I remember saying, "I'll come with you; don't drag me; I have a lame foot." But I was jerked down the steps and away into the dark. I didn't have my feet on the ground; I guess that saved me....

We were rushed into a large room that we found opened on a long hall with brick dungeons on each side. "Punishment cells" is what they call them. They are dungeons. Mine was filthy; it had no window save a little slit at the top and no furniture but a sheet-iron bed and an open toilet flushed from outside the cell....

I saw Dorothy Day brought in. She is a very slight girl. The two men were twisting her arms above her head. Then suddenly they lifted her up and banged her down over the arm of an iron bench—twice. As they ran me past she was lying there with her arms out, and I heard one of the men yell, "The—suffrager!" My mother ain't no suffrager. I'll put you through—."...

The door was barred from top to bottom. The walls were brick cemented over. It was bitter cold. Mrs. Cosu would not let me lie on the floor. She put me on the couch and stretched out on the floor. We had only lain there a few minutes trying to get our breath when Mrs. Lewis, doubled over and handled like a sack of something, was literally thrown in by two men. Her head struck the iron bed as she fell.

We thought she was dead. She didn't move. We were crying over her as we lifted her to the bed and stretched her out, when we heard Miss Burns call: "Where is Mrs. Lewis?"

Mrs. Cosu called out, "They've just thrown her in here." We were roughly told by the guard not to dare speak again, or we would be put in straight- jackets. We were so terrified, we kept very still. Mrs. Lewis was not unconscious; she was only stunned. But Mrs. Cosu was desperately ill as the night wore on. She had a bad heart attack, and then vomiting. We called and called. We asked them to send our doctor because we thought she was dying; there was a woman guard and a man in the corridor, but they paid no attention. A cold wind blew in on us from the outside, and we all lay there shivering and only half conscious until early morning. . . .

I was released on the sixth day, and passed the dispensary as I came out. There were a group of my friends, Mrs. Brannan and Mrs. Morey and several others. They had on coarse striped dresses and big grotesque heavy shoes. I burst into tears as they led me away, my term having expired. I didn't want to desert them like that, but I had done all I could.

Source: *The Suffragist,* December 1, 1917.

**Vocabulary:**
dispensary = hospital or infirmary

**Consider this:**

Summarize the reasons given for the author's view on arresting pickets.

# Why Arresting Pickets is Stupid
### A Word of Advice for the Administration

When President Wilson's administration ordered the arrest of the suffrage pickets—and of course the police have taken their orders in this matter directly from the White House—the administration did a very stupid thing. Mr. Wilson for a moment forgot that the proper answer to words is words, and that any person of government which answers words with force substitutes tyranny for freedom.

From a political standpoint it is always stupid to forsake an appearance of justice. Impatience, no doubt moved the President to order the picketing stopped. He was irritated.

. . . . . . . . . . . . . . . . . . . . . . . . . . . . . . . . . . . .

Arresting pickets is stupid for the following reasons:

It is a violation of the spirit, and probably the letter, of that section of the Clayton law which declares that peaceful picketing is legal. This law was passed during the first year of President Wilson's first term and he had declared himself to be in favor of it.

It is a violation of rights which were conceded to the women pickets when they were permitted to picket for nearly five months.

It is a violation of the fundamental right of every citizen of the republic, when not breaking the peace, to be exempt from arrest.

It is a violation of the right of quiet and legal citizens to be exempt from mistrial and imprisonment.

The arrest and jailing of the pickets is a purely political matter. No one should make the mistake of blaming the police, the prosecuting officers or the magistrate. These are merely the machinery which moves when the man at the top presses the button.

Man-handling nice girls is not a pleasant task. It is only a pity that the people at the top did not have to carry out their own orders.

Source: Gilson Gardner, *The Suffragist*, July 7, 1917.

### *Mrs. Catt Assails Pickets.*
Says Women Make Mistake of Using
Tactics Unworthy of Cause.

Mrs. Carrie Chapman Catt, President of the National American Woman Suffrage Association, said yesterday afternoon that the women who were doing the picketing in Washington had made a psychological mistake. None of the women who went to Washington, Mrs. Catt said, were among those who had made records in the past State suffrage campaign.

"The pickets," Mrs. Catt said, "make the psychological mistake of injecting into this stage of the suffrage campaign tactics which are out of accord with it. Every reform, every change of idea in the world passes through three stages—agitation, argument, and surrender. We have passed through the first two stages and entered into the third. The mistake of the pickets is that they have no comprehensive idea of the movement and are trying to work this first stage in the third. We stand on the threshold of final victory, and the only contribution these women make to it is to confuse the public mind."

Officials at the headquarters of the Woman's Party in New York 13 and 15 East Forty-first Street, were receiving news from the pickets from Washington and making arrangements to get Representatives and Senators to work in

**Consider this:**
Why did the pickets make a mistake, according to Mrs. Catt?

**Vocabulary**
accord = agreement
agitation = excitement
comprehensive = complete
tactics = strategy

**Vocabulary**
incensed = outraged

having the women treated as political prisoners and to urge the President to use his influence for the passage of the Federal amendment. The Congressmen to whom special appeals will be made will be those in whose districts the different forty-one pickets arrested on Saturday and others already imprisoned live. Senators William M. Calder and James Wadsworth, Jr., will be interviewed.

Mrs. Frederick Hazard, who is Chairman of the Syracuse District of the party, was in New York yesterday and said that many people in the upper part of the State, including those not in sympathy with picketing, were very much incensed at the long sentences and treatment that the pickets were receiving.

Source: *New York Times*, November 13, 1917.

# Victory
by
Madeleine Meyers

*The symbol of victory for woman's suffrage* (Illustrated by Nina E. Alexander, September 1920)

After the Anthony Amendment was first introduced to the United States Congress on January 10, 1878, it was re-submitted many times throughout the end of the nineteenth and the beginning of the twentieth centuries, but never with success. Victory seemed near when the House of Representatives approved the amendment on January 10, 1918; however, when the Senate failed to agree, women were once again denied the right to vote.

By that time, support for the amendment was beginning to grow even in some of the more conservative sections of the country. Also, women were beginning to ask for a voice in other aspects of their lives. In 1918, women asked the annual convention of the Protestant Episcopal Church in Massachusetts for the right to vote on the convention floor. After a heated dispute, the request was denied.

When the new Congress convened in May of 1919, women once again faced the task of convincing congressmen to vote in favor of equal suffrage for women. Even President Woodrow Wilson cabled Congress from Europe, encouraging them to approve the amendment. "It seems to me that every consideration of justice and of public advantage calls for the immediate adoption of that amendment and its submission forthwith to the legislatures of the several states."

The Anthony Amendment was again approved by the House of Representatives on May 21, 1919. This time, the Senate approved the amendment on June 4. Looking back at that day, Maude Younger, who was in the Senate gallery, commented: "This was the day toward which women had been struggling for more than a half a century! We were in the dawn of woman's political power in America."

After a frantic campaign to get it ratified by two-thirds of the states, Tennessee became the final state needed for ratification on August 18, and it was signed by Governor Roberts on August 24. Although some members of the Tennessee legislature tried to get the decision annulled, Connecticut soon followed, assuring the necessary states. U.S. Secretary of State Colby signed it into law on August 26, 1920, ending 72 years of struggle.

Although it was not signed in the presence of any of those women who had worked so hard to see it passed, celebrations did follow the final approval. Alice Paul celebrated with her co-workers at the headquarters of the National Woman's Party in Washington. Carrie Chapman Catt was met in New York by cheering crowds, brass bands, and a parade up Fifth Avenue. As for the organizations formed to achieve the goal, the National American Woman Suffrage Association soon dissolved into the League of Woman Voters; the National Women's Party is still active.

**Vocabulary:**

climax = crucial turning point

proclamation = announcement

### Colby Proclaims Woman Suffrage

Signs Certificate of Ratification at His Home Without Women Witnesses.

WASHINGTON, Aug. 26.—The half-century struggle for woman's suffrage in the United States reached its climax at 8 o'clock this morning, when Bainbridge Colby, as Secretary of State, issued his proclamation announcing that the Nineteenth Amendment had become a part of the Constitution of the United States.

The signing of the proclamation took place at that hour at Secretary Colby's residence, 1507 K Street Northwest, without ceremony of any kind, and the issuance of the proclamation was unaccompanied by the taking of movies or other pictures, despite the fact that the National Woman's Party, or militant branch of the general suffrage movement, had been anxious to be represented by a delegation of women and to have the historic event filmed for public display and permanent record.

### No Suffrage Leaders See Signing.

None of leaders of the woman suffrage movement was present when the proclamation was signed.

"It was quite tragic," declared Mrs. Abby Scott Baker of the National Woman's Party. "This was the final culmination of the women's fight, and, women, irrespective of factions, should have been allowed to be present when the proclamation was signed. However, the women of America have fought a big fight and nothing can take from them their triumph."

Source: *New York Times*, August 27, 1920.

**Consider this:**
Why do you think women were not invited to be present when the proclamation was signed?

Why were no photographs taken?

**Vocabulary:**
culmination = climax
irrespective = despite

43

# Sixty-sixth Congress of the United States of America;

## At the First Session,

Begun and held at the City of Washington on Monday, the nineteenth day of May, one thousand nine hundred and nineteen.

---

# JOINT RESOLUTION

Proposing an amendment to the Constitution extending the right of suffrage to women.

---

*Resolved by the Senate and House of Representatives of the United States of America in Congress assembled (two-thirds of each House concurring therein),* That the following article is proposed as an amendment to the Constitution, which shall be valid to all intents and purposes as part of the Constitution when ratified by the legislatures of three-fourths of the several States.

"ARTICLE ————.

"The right of citizens of the United States to vote shall not be denied or abridged by the United States or by any State on account of sex.

"Congress shall have power to enforce this article by appropriate legislation."

*F. H. Gillett*

*Speaker of the House of Representatives.*

*Thos. R. Marshall*

*Vice President of the United States and*
*President of the Senate.*

*The 19th Amendment* (Courtesy of the National Archives)

## The Problem of Women's Freedom

The problem of women's freedom is how to arrange the world so that women can be human beings, with a chance to exercise their infinitely varied gifts in infinite ways, instead of being destined by the accident of their sex to one field of activity—housework and child-raising. And second, if and when they choose housework and child-raising to have that occupation recognized by the world as work, requiring a definite economic reward and not merely entitling the performer to be dependent on some man. I can agree that women will never be great until they achieve a certain emotional freedom, a strong healthy egotism, and some unpersonal source of joy—that is this inner sense we cannot make women free by changing her economic status.

Source: Crystal Eastman, *Now We Can Begin* (December, 1920). Found on web site: http://www.spartacus.schoolnet.co.uk/USAsuffrage.htm.

**Consider this:**

What does the author mean by the last sentence quoted here?

Do you agree?

## Liberation Yesterday
### by Marylin Bender

…the past contains the unresolved question of the future. Is the women's rights movement destined to continue as the greatest talkathon of modern times or will it achieve the transformation of modern society and the genuine equality between the sexes that has been its constant goal?

From Lucretia Mott to Betty Friedan, feminists have been indefatigably verbal. Everything said today has indeed been said and written before: In 1837, Susan B. Anthony, then a 17-year-old teacher, was asking for equal pay for

**Vocabulary:**

indefatigably = tirelessly

45

**Consider this:**

In what ways are women still fighting for equal rights today?


**Vocabulary:**

spasmodic = intermittant

women teachers, coeducation and higher education for women.

In 1848, Elizabeth Cady Stanton and other abolitionist women assembled at Seneca Falls, N.Y., and asserted in a declaration of principles that "all men and women are equal."…

"Radical reform" was what Miss Anthony and Mrs. Stanton expected their magazine, *The Revolution*, to further in 1868. "Educated suffrage, irrespective of sex or color; equal pay to women for equal work; eight hours labor; abolition of standing armies and party despotism. Down with politicans—Up with the people!" they asked in language that seems startingly contemporary.

But then feminism has always seemed visionary. It has always swung from revolution to reaction, propelled on spasmodic bursts of energy toward astonishing achievement before subsiding into compromise and indifference.…

It always had its separatists, starting with Lucy Stone, who kept her name after marrying Henry Blackwell in 1855.… There were always the militants and the conservatives, the radicals and the reformers, the single-minded suffragists and broad-gauge social reconstructionists.… Because of the bitter rivalry between Alice Paul and Carrie Chapman Catt, neither witnessed the signing of the suffrage proclamation. The suffrage triumph was a landmark for decline. Many feminists, old and new, acknowledged that counterrevolution followed.

Source: *New York Times*, August 21, 1970.

# Research Activities/Things to Do

- Why do you think that the right to vote was given to former slaves after the Civil War, but not to women?

- Although many men scoffed at the Women's Rights Convention held in Seneca Falls, New York in 1848, James Gordon Bennett of the *New York Herald* said: "We are much mistaken if Lucretia [Mott] would not make a better President than some of those who have lately tenanted the White House." To whom do you think he was referring, and why?

- Point out the differences in the Declaration of Independence and Lucretia Mott's Declaration of Sentiments excerpted on pages 7 to 9.

- In 1872, Susan B. Anthony, her sister, and a few friends were arrested for voting illegally. Act as her defense lawyer, and give your closing argument supporting her right to vote.

- In 1878, Susan B. Anthony proposed what came to be known as the "Anthony Amendment" at a senate committee hearing. It took 42 years before it was made part of the Constitution. Why do you think that legislation that has to do with women takes so long to be passed? Are men today still trying to act as decision-makers on women's issues? Explain.

- Why were there mixed feelings at the Akron, Ohio women's convention about Sojourner Truth's participation?

- During 1910 to 1920, parades became the new tactic for the suffragettes. How do those parades compare with the use of television or the internet, today? Do you know of any recent parades organized to promote political issues?

- During the struggle for women's rights, a strong rivalry developed between Carrie Chapman Catt and Alice Paul. Trace the roots of their dispute that divided the National American Woman Suffrage Association in 1914.

## Sample Graphic

*In Wyoming Territory, on December 10, 1869, women were invested with "all the political rights, duties, franchises, and responsibilities of male citizens." This artwork first appeared in* Frank Leslie's Weekly, *November 24, 1888, with the caption "Wyoming's Voters in Skirts."*

- Analyze the artwork using the worksheet on page 51.

- In 1869, without the support of the activist women from the East, the pioneer women of the Wyoming Territory became the first women in America to win the unlimited right to vote. Do some independent research to determine their rationale for demanding this right.

- Ask an elderly woman from the neighborhood or from your family if she remembers her mother or grandmother talking about the women's vote issue.

- If women had had the right to vote from the time of the colonists, how might things have been different in our nation's history? Consider government, family life, careers, etc.

- Can U. S. citizens demonstrate and picket peacefully today, without fear of being arrested, like the suffragettes?

- Compare the cartoon of picketing on page 31 with the photo on page 33. Which do you find more effective? Why?

- Write a poem or a short story about women working for suffrage.

_____

_____

_____

_____

_____

_____

_____

_____

_____

_____

_____

_____

_____

_____

_____

_____

_____

## *Sample Cartoon*

1975, *Chicago Sun Times*

- Interpet the following cartoon on a current women's issue, The Equal Rights Amendment, using the worksheet on page 51.

# *Analyzing Graphics, Cartoons, and Photos Worksheet*

Some or all of the following will help you to analyze an historic photo, cartoon, or other type of graphic. Use the worksheet to jot down notes about the piece being evaluated.

1. **What is the subject matter?**

2. **What details provide clues?**

   ❑ scene          ❑ buildings          ❑ people
   ❑ clothing        ❑ artifacts          ❑ time of day
   ❑ style of graphic  ❑ written message    ❑ season
   ❑ B&W/color

3. **Can you determine the location?     The intended audience?**

4. **What is the date? If there is no date, can you guess the period?**

5. **What is the purpose of the poster, ad, artwork, photo, cartoon, etc.?**

   ❑ private use      ❑ recording an event   ❑ propaganda
   ❑ art             ❑ advertising          ❑ Other_____

6. **Describe the tone (mood) of the picture?**

7. **Are there clues which tell you if the creator was sympathetic to the topic or cause?**

8. **Can you tell anything about the point of view of the graphic?**

   ❑ social          ❑ political           ❑ educational
   ❑ recreational     ❑ sales tool

9. **What details make this piece effective or ineffective?**

10. **Explain the message in your own words.**

11. **Are any symbols used in the graphic? Are they verbal or visual? Describe what each symbol represents.**

    <u>Object</u>                    <u>Symbolizes</u>

# Written Document

Mrs. Minor of Missouri asked the Supreme Court to reconsider woman's right to vote. Below is an excerpt from Chief Justice Morrison R. Waite's opinion of the court. His main concern was whether or not women, as citizens, had the right to vote under the 14th Amendment.

## *Minor v. Happersett (March 30, 1875)*

...When the Federal Constitution was adopted, all the States, with the exception of Rhode Island and Connecticut, had constitutions of their own.... Upon all examination of these constitutions we find that in no State were all citizens permitted to vote....

Women were excluded from suffrage in nearly all the States by the express provision of their constitutions and laws....

No new State has ever been admitted to the Union which has conferred the right of suffrage upon women, and this has never been considered a valid objection to her admission. On the contrary,...the right of suffrage was withdrawn from women as early as 1807 in the State of New Jersey, without any attempt to obtain the interference of the United States to prevent it....

Certainly if the courts can consider any question settled, this is one. For nearly ninety years the people have acted upon the idea that the Constitution, when it conferred citizenship, did not necessarily confer the right of suffrage. If uniform practice long continued can settle the construction of so important an instrument as the Constitution of the United States confessedly is, most certainly it has done here. Our province is to decide what the law is, not to declare what it should be.... No argument as to woman's need of suffrage can be considered. We can only act upon her rights as they exist. It is not for us to look at the hardship of withholding. Our duty is at an end if we find it is within the power of a State to withold.

Being unanimously of the opinion that the Constitution of the United States does not confer the right of suffrage upon any one, and that the constitutions and laws of the several States which commit that important trust to men alone are not necessarily void, we affirm the judgment.

- According to this decision, what entities have the power to confer the right to vote?

- Use the worksheet on page 53 to evaluate this document.

# *Written Document Worksheet*

Based on Worksheet from *Teaching with Documents,*
National Archives and Records Administration

1. **Type of document:**

   ❏ Newspaper      ❏ Diary      ❏ Advertisement

   ❏ Letter      ❏ Ship Manifest      ❏ Deed

   ❏ Memo      ❏ Journal      ❏ Other_____

2. **Unique Characteristics of the Document:**

   ❏ Interesting Stationery    ❏ "RECEIVED" stamp    ❏ Unusual Fold Marks

   ❏ Handwritten    ❏ "CLASSIFIED" stamp    ❏ Written notations

   ❏ Official Seal    ❏ Other stamp_____    ❏ Other_____

3. **Date(s) of Document:**          ❏ No Date

4. **Author of Document:**          **Position:**

5. **For what audience was the document written?**

6. **Key Information** *(In your opinion, what are the 3 most important points of the document?)*

   a.

   b.

   c.

7. **Why do you think the document was written?**

8. **Choose a quote from the document that helped you to know why it was written:**

9. **Write down two clues which you got from the document that tell you something about life in the U.S. at the time the document was written:**

10. **Write a question to the author that you feel is unanswered in the document:**

11. **What do you think the response to the document was?**

# Poem

## *Woman Unsexed By The Vote*
### *by Alice Duer Miller*

Source: Alice Duer Miller, "Poet Laureate" of the suffrage movement, quoted in *Tennessee Women, Past and Present* by Wilma Dykeman.

> It doesn't unsex her to toil in a factory
> Minding the looms from the dawn till the night;
> To deal with a schoolful of children refractory
> Doesn't unsex her in anyone's sight;
> Work in a store—where her back aches inhumanly—
> Doesn't unsex her at all, you will note,
> But think how exceedingly rough and unwomanly
> Woman would be if she happened to vote!
>
> To sweat in a laundry that's torrid and torrider
> Doesn't subtract from her womanly charm;
> And scrubbing the flags in an echoing corridor
> Doesn't unsex her—so where is the harm?
>
> It doesn't unsex her to nurse us with bravery,
> Loosing death's hand from its grip in the throat;
> But ah! how the voices grow quivery, quavery,
> Wailing: "Alas, 'twill unsex her to vote!"
>
> She's feminine still, when she juggles the crockery,
> Bringing you blithely the order you give;
> Toil in a sweatshop where life is a mockery
> Just for the pittance on which she can live—
> That doesn't seem to unsex her a particle
> "Labor is noble"—so somebody wrote—
> But ballots are known as a dangerous article
> Woman's unsexed if you give her the vote!

- Evaluate this poem using the worksheet on page 55.

## *Analyzing Songs/Poems Worksheet*

1. **Type of song document:**
   ❑ Sheet music          ❑ Recording          ❑ Printed Lyrics only
   ❑ Other_____

2. **Time period from which the song or poem comes:**

3. **Date(s) on Song:**
   ❑ No Date              ❑ Copyright

4. **Composer:**          **Lyricist:**          **Poet:**

5. **For what audience was the piece written?**

6. **Key Information** (In your opinion, what is the message of the song/poem?)

7. **Do you think the song/poem was spontaneously written?**

8. **Choose a quote from the piece that helped you to know why it was written:**

9. **Write down two clues which you got from the words that tell you something about life in the U. S. at the time it was written:**

10. **What is the mood of the music or poetry?**

11. **Do you think the song/poem was used for propaganda? If so, describe the propaganda:**

12. **Does the wording have any "secret message" or symbolic meaning?**

13. **Is the song or poem still being sung or read on a regular basis today?**

# Suggested Further Reading

The books listed below are suggested readings in American literature, which tie in with the *Researching American History Series*. The selections were made based on feedback from teachers and librarians currently using them in interdisciplinary classes for students in grades 5 to 12. Of course there are many other historical novels that would be appropriate to tie in with the titles in this series.

## Woman's Suffrage

* *Lucretia Mott: Friend of Justice*, Kem Knapp Sawyer - EL/M (biography)

* *Long Way to Go: A Story of Women's Right to Vote*, Zibby Oneal - EL/M

* *Feminism and Suffrage: The Emergence of an Independent Women's Movement in America*, E. C. DuBois - HS (nonfiction)

* *The Road to Freedom: A Play about Sojourner*, Sharon Fennessey - EL/M

* *One Woman, One Vote, Rediscovering the Woman Suffrage Movement*, Marjorie Spruill Wheeler - M/HS

For information on these and other titles from Discovery Enterprises, Ltd., call or write to: Discovery Enterprises, Ltd., 31 Laurelwood Drive, Carlisle, MA 01741  Phone: 978-287-5401  Fax: 978-287-5402